I0463993

Let's Put the
REAL
Back into
REAL
ESTATE

Jim Keogh

Copyright © 2014 Jim Keogh.

All rights reserved. No part of this book may be used or reproduced by
any means, graphic, electronic, or mechanical, including photocopying,
recording, taping or by any information storage retrieval system
without the written permission of the publisher except in the case
of brief quotations embodied in critical articles and reviews.

Archway Publishing books may be ordered
through booksellers or by contacting:

Archway Publishing
1663 Liberty Drive
Bloomington, IN 47403
www.archwaypublishing.com
1-(888)-242-5904

Because of the dynamic nature of the Internet, any web addresses or
links contained in this book may have changed since publication and
may no longer be valid. The views expressed in this work are solely those
of the author and do not necessarily reflect the views of the publisher,
and the publisher hereby disclaims any responsibility for them.

Any people depicted in stock imagery provided by Thinkstock are
models, and such images are being used for illustrative purposes only.
Certain stock imagery © Thinkstock.

ISBN: 978-1-4808-0910-9 (sc)
ISBN: 978-1-4808-0927-7 (e)

Library of Congress Control Number: 2014911889

Printed in the United States of America.

Archway Publishing rev. date: 07/09/2014

Dedication

I would like to dedicate this book to Carl Wise, former mayor of the city of Canton, OH and real estate broker for his fatherly mentoring skills. Not only did he teach me the basic skills in my formative years in real estate, but he handed over some sweet deals for me to cut my teeth on. I worked full time for him for three years and I thoroughly enjoyed his guidance and making money with him.

I would also like to thank my wife, Deloris, for standing by me and supporting me in the real estate business.

Lastly, thank you to Danielle Hayduk, who helped me make some money, and without whose support and skill I wouldn't have written this book.

Contents

Introduction ix

What's Real and Not Real in Real Estate 1

Who Should and Should Not Be in Real Estate..... ... 11

The Importance of Education 17

Wholesaling 19

The Deal I Had The Most Fun With 29

Private Money Lending vs. Hard Money Lending.... 33

Buying Real Estate at Auction 39

Rehabbing Ideas 43

What To Look For In A Property 47

Keys to My Success 51

This Is Not A Negative Book 55

Introduction

Why I Got Into Real Estate

When I was a kid I saw our landlord. I saw our landlord's car, and I liked it. I saw our landlord's house, and I liked it. After I got married I told my wife I wanted to buy a duplex. So I got my real estate license and for fourteen years I worked my day job and I worked part time—in real estate.

My parents never owned a house, but I could see why it was better to buy and have tenants to pay my mortgage than to rent. As soon as I could I bought my first rental property: a duplex I moved my bride into two years after we were married.

My wife, Doloris, didn't know what she was in for when we first started dating. Little by little she got used to the idea that I was going to be making a career in real estate. She embraced my dream, or at least she offered no resistance. As a matter of fact, she waited patiently for new carpeting in our home while I bought another rental property. In a sense, she enabled me to become the real estate compulsive buyer I have become.

I guess there could be worse compulsions than that. After thirty years of investing, buying and holding, I diversified and took on lending. Over the past twenty years I have made over sixty loans, allowing investors to change the face of entire neighborhoods.

I come from a city of 110,000 in the Northeastern corner of the state of Ohio, Canton, home of the Football Hall of Fame. Located in Stark County, approximately sixty miles South of Cleveland, Canton has a long history of manufacturing, sports enthusiasm and is a nice place to raise a family.

My father was a salesman for International Trucks, and my mother retired from the S.S. Kresge five and dime store (they also had a dollar side inside the store) after thirty nine years. They were hard workers, but they never really made any large amounts of money. Although many would have considered us poor, I never realized it. My basic needs were always taken care of. When I was nineteen I gave them $2,000 as a downpayment on their first home, a house they bought on land contract from a rehabber.

For me, real estate was a means to the lifestyle I wanted, and since I had that salesman mentality, I thought that being a real estate agent would be the best way for me to achieve my goals. So in addition to my day job at Buxbaun Rubber Company, where I worked as a shipping clerk, I sold real estate part time for four years.

For two years I weighed the pros and cons of leaving that day job. With two small children at home I was afraid of leaving us exposed without health insurance. Eventually my passion won as selling real estate became too attractive to ignore.

After working another two years as a full time real estate agent for Carl Wise, I got my brokers' license and started a new agency with three others: a builder, another broker and an insurance broker. Eventually we bought the first Century 21 franchise in Stark County and grew it into a sales force of thirty-five. We sold new construction for the builder and we were the test market for Republic Steel houses in a brand new allotment.

Four years of playing father to my sales force took its toll on me, and I had the good fortune to get out just before interest rates skyrocketed and the new housing market dried up in the late sixties. Luckily for me, I had already purchased a number of rentals which helped me through rough times.

Shortly thereafter I took what I thought was going to be a temporary job at the Stark County Auditor's office in downtown Canton in the old San Francis Hotel. As a

Senior Staff Appraiser, I verified tax values for formal complaints and was responsible for the largest territory (some forty thousand parcels). I was relieved when I was offered early retirement after some seventeen long years. Finally I was able to give my full attention to a neglected real estate career.

What's Real and Not
Real in Real Estate

*The first deal is the most important deal--because
if you scare yourself out of that first deal, you may
never do another.—James Keogh*

My first deal was a converted duplex that had seen
better days. The carpet was worn thin, the paint
was scuffed up, it needed some serious sprucing up, and
it was dirty. I bought it for $7,500, borrowing $1,500
from my mother for the down payment and getting a
mortgage from a local bank for the rest.

I cleaned the duplex up, but I never even thought of
replacing the carpet or repainting the walls. I rented
the downstairs for sixty-five dollars a month and the
upstairs for forty-five dollars. By the time the first tenant
moved out, he owed me three hundred dollars in back
rent. When I went after him, he filed bankruptcy, and
eventually I received three dollars a month for a while.

A few years later, I called in an auctioneer and sold the

building for $4,500. So, you would say, I sold it at a loss. But I made some money in rent for those years. Could I have done better? Probably. Live and learn.

So what was real to me was that I collected rent and made some money. What was also real was that I let my tenant live there rent-free for almost half a year. What was even more real is that my building didn't appreciate while I owned it.

Money ... Money ... Money ...

Myth

Once you buy a property, you will have money right away and your property will generate positive cash flow. Maybe that holds true if you purchase a property with cash and you have no major repairs.

Reality

Real estate is like a baby. It needs its diaper changed. It needs to be fed and taken care of. So you better have money to buy those diapers and food. A house is like a kid. It needs things. And just like a child who matures and grows into his own personality, it takes time for a property to settle into its own routine. For the first three to four months, things are a little unsettled: you are feeling your way with your tenants and they are feeling you out, maybe testing you, pushing your limits. You are establishing your own position as landlord and need to hand-hold your tenants until they get used to paying their rent and juggling their bills. This house requires your attention—a lot of your attention.

One of my friends, Stanley, found this out the hard way. Stanley wanted to make a splash in real estate. He bought fifteen houses in three months. He was so preoccupied juggling the fifteen properties that he couldn't give them the proper attention and take the time to season each one of them. His properties never settled down. He had too many vacancies, which affected his cash flow. He had too many problems, too many maintenance issues, and not enough money or time to devote to each of them. He didn't have enough money for the diapers he needed. A year later Stanley lost all his properties to bankruptcy.

Flocking to the Gurus ...
Looking for Money, Money, Money

Myth

It's as easy as "Do as I say. Do what I tell you to do, and you will prosper as I did." Isn't that the way a lot of gurus come across? "It's easy to do, and here is a blueprint of how to get there."

Reality

You and only you will be responsible for your success. If you really want to be successful, you will overcome the problems that need to be overcome. You will find the right way. You will keep working or getting advice and education until it all comes together and you are successful.

Better not to quit your day job. At least not until you've mastered the program. If you do what your guru tells you, you will have a greater degree of success. But you are probably going to need help. After all, if you were a clone of the guru, you might be teaching the class yourself, instead of sitting in the audience as an attendee. So you need a few key ingredients that will sustain you to keep going. Let's face it: during the program, you got all riled up. You bought into the program, didn't you? You coughed up the big bucks, took home the package, popped the CDs into your player, called up your wife, shared the news, and got a big "What? You spent how much?"

So a little deflated, a little less sure of yourself, you looked back at the package and decided that you had better find the help you need to *show her!* Luckily, you also read back over your notes and there was a line with a big fat star you had drawn next to it: "Get involved with your local REIA (Real Estate Investors' Association)."

The REIA. This is where it all really starts. You get to rub elbows with the movers and shakers (we'll call them the M&S) who know how things work. The M&S give advice (most of the time for free). The M&S are local, so they give advice that is pertinent to your geographical area (as opposed to the guru who may live three states away). Your M&S know the local rules and regulations and the local customs.

As far as I'm concerned, joining your local REIA group means less money invested, and the mentoring is as good as or better than the national guru. Plus you get ongoing advice and motivation. If you don't have a local REIA group, form one yourself.

Get Rich Quick

Myth

Plug into a system, the right system, and you will prosper.

Reality

Don't quit your day job. Did I already say that? In all seriousness, you must have a real job. You need steady income to keep up with your living expenses. You don't want to ruin your credit, because it makes it harder to get a loan, and it doesn't look good to have a property foreclosed on, to be forced into bankruptcy, or to stand in line in front of the food bank with your tenants.

To every person who comes to me for advice, I have a few questions that may shed some light on their strengths and weaknesses.

Q. How much money do you have to invest?

If that person answers, "None. Guru X claims I can buy real estate with no money," then I will patiently explain to them that you have to find a source of money in order to wheel and deal in the real estate business.

You can look for owner-financed properties, from motivated sellers, but in many cases, if the seller is willing to finance a property, it may not be prime real estate. If you are going to buy real estate with no money to back you up, then you will probably wind up with junk properties. And in that case, a really important question to ask yourself is this: "Can I sell it tomorrow and get my cash out of it?"

And let's be realistic. Somewhere in the process, you are going to need some cash, if only to pay the insurance at closing.

Q. What kind of experience do you have in real estate?

When I purchased my first investment property, I had little real experience in real estate. I had traveled a little all over to seminars and had listened to a few programs, because I knew I had to spend some time and money on education. Somehow, though, I hadn't heard of REIAs, and it was a while before I actually stumbled upon the Akron group.

In spite of this little practical experience, I still felt I was way ahead of George, who came to me because he had a dilemma. George owned three properties, but at the time, he came to seek advice. He had no money, no job, and his properties weren't holding their own. The first property he bought with seller financing, and he sold it for the same amount he had purchased it for. He wanted to sell the others, but he realized that he owed more on them than they were worth.

The clincher was that in addition to owning properties that were costing him money, he had racked up $60,000 on his credit card in courses and boot camps. He felt fortunate to have found another credit company that he could transfer that balance to. None of it sounded good to me.

Another common answer I get to the question about real estate experience is this: "I own my own home." Do realize that owning a home does not mean you are experienced in investing in real estate.

Q. Why do you want to get into this business?

- I read a book on it and it sounds like a great way to make money.

- I bought some courses and listened to them, but I haven't done anything with them yet. I think it's time to get started.

I have often heard people say that they are ready to jump in with both feet. I often go the extra mile and present them with a wholesale deal that I think they would be foolish to refuse. Most of the time, they don't take it. Five years later, some of them might even think back and kick themselves for not taking the opportunity.

Q. Do you have your team put together?

In most cases, they have no idea what I am even talking about.

Let's talk about who you should have on your team.

a. a lawyer
b. an accountant

c. a Realtor
d. an array of contractors to handle maintenance issues
e. a banker/financial institution
f. a management company (in which case they will take care of d)
g. a home inspector

Interview your prospective team members, prequalifying them based on their level of success and experience. Ask your fellow investors for recommendations, and do your due diligence.

Q. Have you or will you join a REIA group?

You guessed right! The only answer is YES.

Q. How do you determine the purchase price of a piece of property?

A lot of new investors don't really know how to do this, so when I ask them, I hear,

"I don't know, but I would like to learn how." or,

"I rely on my realtor.", or,

"I don't really have any experience, I just make an offer."

You should really look at as many properties as you can. The search for a realtor who is investor-friendly can take a while, but when you find one you should be able to get some reliable information.

Talk to other investors about the area and their experience in that area. One thing I know is that there is one thing we all share: we never turn down an opportunity to look at real estate. So ask other investors to tag along and give you their opinion.

Who Should and Should Not Be in Real Estate….

Josh, a friend of mine, had toyed with the idea of buying real estate for a while. Eventually I got him to buy a duplex. It seemed to be the perfect property for him to try out his investor wings. To my surprise, two years after the fact he called me up to tell me his doctor was recommending that he sell the house because it was affecting his health.

This was a well built duplex in a very nice neighborhood. There were no maintenance issues out of the ordinary. His tenants were paying their rent on time. But Josh had blown his pride of ownership way out of proportion. He was so emotionally involved with the house that he was there all the time, keeping the lawn manicured, the weeds tamed, the shrubs trimmed. When he wasn't there he worried about it, lost sleep over it, treated it like he lived there.

Poor Josh, he was the impersonation of who should not be in real estate. You just can't get emotionally attached to a property. It will cloud your judgment, so even if you find the house that reminds you of your childhood home, that is not reason enough to buy it. And unless it meets other criteria that will actually generate cash flow, you should steer away from any property that pulls at your heart strings.

Leave your homeowner mentality at home...
When you buy a house that you yourself are going to live in, you usually have a list of must-haves, and then you usually let yourself be WOWed by some additional features. Then, before you know it, you're in love. You can't stop thinking about that house. You visualize where the flat screen TV is going. You can see how you are going to arrange your bedroom.

While falling in love with your own home is part of the process called *homeownership*, you cannot transfer that emotional attachment to your investment property choices. Look at the moment when you submit your offer. How much would you let your emotional attachment sway the dollar amount on your offer? If you get into a bidding war, will your emotional attachment push you to offer more than the property is worth?

You have to be somewhat of an adrenaline junkie... and enjoy a good challenge.
Finding a property you are interested in brings on a rush of excitement; there is no denying it. And although it can't quite compare to sky-diving or a good game of

laser tag, it is enough to keep some of us going. There is the rush that comes when you realize that it's a good deal. Then there is the rush when you submit your offer and the rush when it is accepted, or countered.

The challenges in this business are never-ending, and I'd venture to say that every real estate transaction presents its own challenge. Every deal teaches you something new—details can get in the way and you need to decide what you are going to do about a situation you had not anticipated. Do you pull the plug or forge ahead? At the drop of a hat you need to put on your thinking cap to resolve a problem.

Work at real estate like it's a job...

If you're not interested in putting out the vegetables, you aren't going to sell any. If your local supermarket clerk sits in the back of the store, too lazy or uninterested to set up the produce display, the supermarket isn't going to sell any produce. You have to be out there getting the word out, doing the rounds, and treating it like it is your full time job—even if it's not. There is no such thing as *dabbling* in real estate.

Who should definitely, positively not be in real estate...

People who ask for advice but never take it. You know who they are. They corner you at the end of a meeting to ask you in what area they should buy rentals. You give them your perspective, tell them what areas to avoid at all costs, then you learn that they bought a rental in the three gun neighborhood you told them to avoid. They may even have bought a second one there.

They are the same ones who hire a home inspector before they buy, listen to the inspector's list of issues, listen to the inspector say that they should run from this one, but turn around and buy it anyway.

People who buy junk properties probably should also stay away from real estate investing. They are the ones who can't pass up a good deal. They will tell you, "The owner only wants $5,000 for this house. Can you believe it?" These investors don't get the *too good to be true* concept.

They are also the ones who wind up with owner financing deals where they don't know exactly what the terms of their contract are. Four years, maybe five, not sure what the interest rate is, or how much goes towards principal, or even sometimes what the final purchase price is. That is no way to run a business.

Who should be in real estate...
• Someone with the ability to talk to people. They should possess a degree of boldness, and be willing to talk to strangers. *A people-person is a good fit.*

• Real estate investors, just like expert salesmen, concentrate on problem-solving, so uncovering someone's hot-buttons is essential. *A problem-solver is a good fit.*

• Negotiating skills are an integral part of the business. Listening to what the other party says, and does not say will get you further than just throwing an offer out there. *An expert negotiator is key.*

• Someone who possesses a certain degree of education in some aspect of real estate. Either you have gone for formal training of some kind, or you have tackled the realms of self-teaching, a serious investor will probably have started with some education. *A motivated student is a good start.*

The Importance of Education

Either you go to college, get hired into a company, in debt, and quickly get capped out at your salary range or you can join a REIA where you will learn how to buy and sell real estate. REIAs are an investors' version of a college education in the field of real estate.

In real estate there is no cap as to how much you can make. You can make as much as you want. When gas goes up to $5/gallon, the college grad will have to stop buying bread and milk so he can get to work, but the real estate investor just needs to make another deal to make up for an increase in expenses.

I also have job security--I can't get fired. I work with my brain, so I just keep thinking!

Should you get a college degree to make money in real estate? No. I don't think it is necessary.

Attend as many educational programs dealing with real estate as you can. The more you attend the more benefits and opportunities you will identify.

Most successful people in the world have found a need and supply that need. Everyone needs a roof over their head, a place to sleep. How smart do you have to be to supply that?

Make your own luck. Find a mentor, get out there, be persistent, figure out a way to get where you want to go.

Wholesaling

Wholesaling is the investor's tool for turning over a property without improvements. With a wholesale deal you can either make quick cash or mark it up and hold a mortgage.

No matter what your method is, you need to have a program that includes a stable of buyers. You develop that stable by going to your existing pool of investors, or a REIA group, for example. My personal list of buyers comes primarily from the Stark County or the Akron Canton REIA groups.

You will need sources of money that you or your buyers may use if you don't have your own funds or access to funds.

In order to make a wholesale deal attractive to your investor buyers and make money yourself, you need to find bargains with room for a wholesale deal, in other words, a good buy to attach a profit onto.

The potential profit is what you deem your time to be

worth. I like to make 10K because you need room for the investor buyer to make his money too. So I make 10K for signing a few pieces of paper, looking at a house or two and showing it once or twice.

Most often I take a potential buyer who I think might be a fit for that house at the same time as I look at it for the first time.

Since a new investor needs to learn the skills of the trade, you need to get an education on how to wholesale… where do you go? Again, to the REIA group! There may be 100 courses out there on wholesaling, and then there is the school of hard knocks.

If our buyer is experienced, they know the cost of rehabbing and getting the house back on the market. If you are more knowledgeable than they are, you need to protect your buyer. If you don't have that expertise, hire someone who can help you out. Either someone who has been in the biz for a long time or an honest, reliable, home inspector who can point out some of the problem areas.

In wholesaling you can't be greedy. There has to be room for the investor buyer to pay for repairs and still make a profit.

Caution: everything depends on the location and the exit strategy. If they are keeping the property as a rental, make sure the property will appraise high enough to pay you back if you are carrying the financing.

There is no simple formula, or should I say, you need multiple formulas. Here are your choices:

Cash deals
Carrying back some or all of financing
Advancing money for rehab
Retail buyer wholesale price

Cash deals are simple, once you get your cash, you are no longer in bed with that investor buyer.

Carrying back financing: you can carry back just the purchase price, or the purchase price plus rehab money. In this scenario you are risking more money, assuming you make the right decision on your valuation. If this person can't perform, what recourse do you have? What are the consequences? Will you get your money out of it? Will it be short term, or long term? Will you make your money back?

If wholesaling is your strategy and if that is what you do exclusively, you won't have to worry about toilets and tenants. It does take more work than dealing with tenants or toilets because you have to go back out and find more inventory. You will need to talk to a lot more sellers before you can find a good prospect for a wholesale deal.

You could purchase a number of properties, and hold them, incurring expenses, holding fees, etc. and wait until you have a buyer.

Building inventory...
Options... you can take an option on a property, find a buyer, assign your option for $10,000 (over the property you have under option).

Land contracts... the biggest bugaboo is that you need to have money to tie up houses or buy them.

Take a house that has been on the market for a while, and has not be getting any action, or a seller sitting on two houses, with two payments; you are going to need several months to work on finding a buyer. It depends on all the ingredients being in that mix at the right time.

If you are going to wholesale, go get yourself a few houses, put them on the shelf as inventory. Most importantly, make sure you have a good exit strategy.

I once purchased a house wholesale in Lake township. It had a fenced-in back yard, four car garage, in the Reindeer allotment. I purchased it for $110K, wholesale, in an area where everything else sold for $165K. I anticipated 40K in rehab, but I hadn't taken into account a tenacious pet smell. Just getting rid of the pet odor cost me $50K and took four months.

Originally the only house for sale in the neighborhood, when I was ready to sell it was one of many. There were a ton of houses for sale. I took a loan out on it, rented it out, making money on the equity which I was able to put to work on another house.

*Deloris and Jim Keogh on their wedding day,
June 24, 1961.*

First duplex bought by Keogh in 1963

Deloris made Century 21 jackets for the whole family...

At the Stark County auditor's office as a Senior Staff Appraiser, from 1982 - 1998

Keogh (left) with Senator Scott Oelslager.

What Keogh really wants to be doing...

Keogh's favorite pastime: Jeeping... here waiting for their turn at a Jeep Jamboree in Murphy, N.C.

What really happens at a Jeep Jamboree...

The Deal I Had The Most Fun With

There was a house for sale on 13th Street in Canton, OH. When I went to see the house, my buddy Frank was with me. He noticed that the house next door was vacant, and left his business card in the door, with a note asking if the house might be for sale.

One year to the date, Frank receives a phone call. Frank asked me if I would go over with him to look at the house. We met the owner--he had been raised in that house. He had also started some remodeling but had not done a very good job.

Frank's intention was to buy the house. "We have an interest in your property, but we have to do our homework." we told the owner. As always, we asked the question, "would the owner be interesting in holding some of the financing?". "Absolutely not", the owner answered. We went back to the office, did our homework, and asked the owner to come by the office.

Frank was there. The owner showed up with his girlfriend. I took out the form that I always use. It states the costs associated with the sale of his property if he uses a Realtor, how much rehab costs are and how much he would get out of the sale of the property.

My form starts off with a realistic market value, minus rehab costs, Realtor's commission and closing costs. The bottom line read: $18,740. I slid the paper across the table. I was expecting the owner to hit the ceiling, and take out a few things. Instead, there was no reaction. He handed the paper to his girlfriend. I expected her to hit the ceiling, but once again, there was no reaction. Then he said to me, "We were hoping for more.". "$18,740 is the net," I said. "There are no other expenses. They said they would take it.

"Would you consider taking back some owner financing if you had a credit worthy buyer for a certain amount of time?".

"No, my car got repossessed, I've got some bills," he said, "I have to get it out of hock.

"Well, how much would it take?" I ventured. "$2,000" was his answer.

"I'm thinking about a $2,500 down payment, and you carry the rest for twelve months. Would you be interested in that?" I responded.

"Well, I have to pay off my credit cards." he said. This is where I thought the whole deal was going to go south.

"Well, how much do you owe on your credit cards?" I asked.

"$300", he answered. I had to refrain from bursting out laughing.

"We can give you $3,000 down and 6% interest for twelve months." I countered.

"OK" he said. We had a deal, Frank wanted to wholesale the house anyway. I had been working with a 14 year old boy, Chris, who asked me if I would mentor him. I told Frank I might have someone to buy his house. I called Chris, made an appointment with him and his dad. I told him to do his homework to find out how much to offer on the house. He offered a little less than Frank wanted for the house, about $24K.

Before we even closed the deal, a real estate agent wanted to show the house. His client made an offer, enabling Chris to make a $6K profit. Today, my young protégé has three rentals managed by a property management company and is on his way to being a successful real estate investor.

Private Money Lending vs. Hard Money Lending

Private money is usually less expensive to borrow. It comes from relatives, friends and acquaintances who might be interested in getting a greater return on their money or savings than they can in the bank or in their IRAs.

It can be a scary thing to lend money to a family member. If you grew up playing with Johnny and he gave you a bloody nose or was a whiney kid, you may have a hard time viewing him as a successful real estate investor who could give you a good return on your money.

How secure can you feel about lending out your money to a total stranger or an acquaintance? Well sometimes more at ease than considering doing a deal with little Johnny.

When you are at a family reunion, you may want to plant a seed by sharing a little background information. Sometimes just mentioning real estate is enough to start the conversation. Those around you want to talk about real estate, or making money in real estate. If I say I'm in the real estate business, they want to talk about it themselves.

"My son is looking to buy a house"

"There is an auction at such and such. Is it a good house to buy?"

They think most people make money in real estate and although they may think they want to be a successful real estate investor themselves they may not have the gumption to do it or the drive to see it through.

This is the most exciting business you could possibly be in. Everyday is different, you will have a lot of fun making money. You will see accomplishments you probably thought you could never achieve. You will be able to help people in ways most people can't. It can be rewarding, difficult, fear-provoking and a natural high all in the same day. It's the story of *do you like to go to work in the morning or don't you?*

I have fun making money along with making friends, business acquaintances, helping people with their physical needs and financial advice. I get the biggest enjoyment out of seeing someone start in the business and grow and turn into a successful real estate investor.

How to get people to lend you money

Talk to everyone even if they don't seem to have money. Talk to your circle of friends and strangers. Tell them you borrow money to fund deals. Educate family members... if they have $40K you can explain to them that at 8% interest they could make more money than through conventional savings avenues. Play with the numbers and put it on paper. If I have x amount of dollars, in how many years of loaning it out can I make it back? Show them how to use their money wisely.

Some people understand the value of long term planning vs. immediate gratification, and some just don't. It can be hard to persuade your niece who wants to buy a new car that if she hangs on to her current car, the sacrifice could bring greater rewards down the line.

A more mature person with a savings account, CD, or money in their mattress will be more reluctant to risk their hard earned savings. The hardest thing is to persuade someone that they should risk their money with you and that their savings are reasonably safe and fairly well secured and you are offering them a higher return. Offer them good protection and show them how the risk is minimized. Tell them about promissory notes if you are the borrower, or cognovit notes if you are the lender.

If you have $50,000 to invest, you can buy $50,000 worth of stock, $50,000 in gold or a $50,000 house. If they all go down to $0 in value, what do you wind up with? A

$50,000 doorstop, $50,000 worth of toilet paper or a house that you can rent for $500 a month. Your house will give you tax advantages as well as monthly income.

Where can they find money to lend out? Equity in their house; they can pull it out at a very inexpensive interest rate. They can re-loan it out to you. You may have to deal with a "don't rock the boat" mentality, maybe mostly from the wife, or woman of the house. But it is a smart business move. Ethnic groups typically help one another out and make sacrifices to have a better life and participate in the American Dream. If one family member does well investing, others may want a piece of the action too.

Locate the person who has a low interest bearing CD, who has recently experienced unfavorable fluctuations in the stock market, who have retirement accounts that could be repositioned to generate greater income. Retirement accounts, like IRAs, 401K, stocks and bonds, may offer a lesser income. A quick thought about stock is that you may feel secure that you just bought stock in a popular company, in six months that very same stock could be useless. You might persuade them to liquidate assets that they don't use, such as a vacation home they hardly enjoy, or an extra automobile, jewelry.

Objections will be part of the process, and if you just remember that objections are actually opportunities, you can use them to your advantage by educating your prospective lender. If they think that real estate is a poor risk right now, show them why it is a good time to invest in real estate. If you were to invest in stock, would you feel more comfortable investing in Tessla motors or Ford? Tessla doesn't have as good a track record. Persuade people you are a good risk...

How much of an interest rate should you offer them? Of course you don't want to take advantage, but if you borrow at 20% you are probably doing yourself a disservice. Offer them market rate, or whatever is amenable to both parties. The more sophisticated they are the higher an interest rate they will want. Make sure that you treat them fairly-- they probably have more where that came from. Take into account the spread you decide you are willing to work with. A spread is the difference between the interest rate you borrow at and the interest rate you lend out at. For instance, if I borrow $10,000 and was happy with a 6% spread, my profit from using other people's money would be $600. Needless to say, the larger or greater the spread, the greater profitability there is.

Hard Money...
Hard because it is more expensive money to borrow, but in most cases a lot easier to acquire than from a conventional lender.

What to expect with hard money...

A sophisticated lender with a set of guidelines that they go by, and there will be very little room for negotiation. It's a take it or leave it situation. It's like a gallon of gasoline. It is priced at a certain price and if you want it you pay for it.

As long as you have credibility it is easy to get a loan. It certainly is a beneficial program for a smart investor. Hard money is not meant for long term financing; you use it to get control of a piece of real estate that you can make some money with. It is a type of bridge financing that you can use to buy something now.

Expensive money affects profitability, so you need to run your numbers to determine if your bottom line is worth the use of this more expensive money. Assuming you borrow from a hard money lender, your profit would only be $8000 vs. $10,000 from a conventional lender at their lower interest rate. Will this be a good deal assuming you have to do the dance for the conventional lender who may or may not lend to you. In the meantime, your deal may vanish with the additional time the conventional lender takes to decide if he will or will not loan you the money.

Personally, there are a lot of people who own a lot of properties today that they would not have owned without my assistance.

Buying Real Estate at Auction

Auctions are an excellent place to purchase investment properties, and the auction block is flooded with properties that are being liquidated as their owners move into assisted living situations. These auctions can offer investors a good opportunity to pick up a choice property.

In this scenario you are not going to make an offer, you bid. One of the downfalls of auctions is that is is easy to get swept up in the momentum and bid over what you have allocated for the property. Sometimes you go in with no idea on how much you are going to spend.

It's a really good idea to go into an auction prepared. Write on a piece of paper what your maximum bid should be. Let's say the property is worth 100K. Take out the price to rehab. Add in taxes, buyer's premium, etc., and that final number will determine what your maximum bid should be.

Try to get inside the property in advance, to see it at your leisure. Most of the time, the auctioneers will only allow you in on the day of the auction. Do your homework, try not to go over the price you have determined.

I don't know how many times my final bid has been accepted, but I have gone overboard a few times. Some auctions charge a 10% buyer's premium, so make sure your paper includes that additional 10%. The auction house requires 15-25% of the purchase price down at the time of the auction. This down payment is nonrefundable. You will have to sign a note or have to put down cash and you will have so much time to close on the property.

A lot of the country hadn't been selling real estate through auctions; you could say we are pioneers in Northeastern OH, trendsetters, in a sense, with some agencies that have been selling real estate at auction for more than 50 years.

Each auction has its own set of circumstances. Some properties go too high. Sometimes a rainy day attracts more bidders than you expect. Try to attend as many as you can and eventually you will pick up a good deal at an auction where there aren't too many people …

What to look for when you do your walk through at an auction…
Usually the auction house has done its due diligence and bidders can take a look at an appraisal, a seller's disclosure, a termite report and other information pertaining to the state of the property. Using these tools can give you a starting point to help you evaluate how much work a

house will need. After 50 years in the business, I can still make mistakes determining the value of a property, but fortunately it has never resulted in a dramatic change of my lifestyle.

I recently purchased a property in Canton, OH, in the southwest for 35K. I didn't actually expect to put 17K into it, but I didn't see everything that was that was wrong with it. The more auctions you can go to, and the more people you can take with you, the more issues with the property will come to light.

Since auctions are great opportunities for investors, you are likely to run into competition from fellow investors as well as from retail buyers. They can drive prices up quickly, since they aren't looking at the property to produce a profit.

The bottom line is simple: you have to be there to be the winner. I have personally picked up 15 to 20 properties at auction.

Rehabbing Ideas

Rehabbing can make you or break you real quick. The biggest problem when you are purchasing a house for rehab is acquiring it at the right price. If you don't have the ability to establish the correct purchase price, you had better seek advice.

Be careful, even more so, because holding a property to rent can bail you out, but it can be a profit or a loss on the rehab. One of the biggest problems is that a lot of people think they can do the work on their own, which results in a lot of the owners' time as well as delays in getting the property back on the market.

Hiring a reliable contractor results in a shorter period of time for the house to be put back on the market, which decreases your holding costs. I am always leary of dragging rehab into a period of winter weather where you property has less possibilities of being sold. I have found that the money you spend on the contracting will come back to you because the property is turned over quicker. If you don't step back and allow the contractor to take over the job, you could be in the way of the contractor getting his job finished because you haven't done your portion of the work or you screw up the timeline.

One of the big bugabooos of rehabbing are the hidden things that are not seen until you start demolition or for the second or third time when you see something you hadn't seen before. Allow for the unknown, or hidden problems that creep up on you. How much should you allow? Depends on the size of the project, the age of the house and your own experience on what to look for.

Location is an extremely important thing especially if you want to sell your property. If you intend to rent, it is still an important factor, but not to the same degree. Rehabbing for resale means more effort put toward giving the property a wow factor that is not necessarily needed for rental properties. Create something over and above your competition.

Figure out your competition when you are buying the house, hopefully those houses will only be your competition.

Three ingredients to having a good listing:

1. Location: you have to have a good location

2. Price

3. Motivation to sell

There are a lot of courses on rehabbing. If you see one that works for you, try it out, spend your money wisely, make it a learning lesson and move on from there. This is without a doubt one of my weakest areas, and I don't even particularly like it, so if I buy with the idea of renting a property out I am not concerned with profitability.

What To Look For In A Property

In real estate, buying, and selling both depend on your exit strategy. What you look for--or what you are on the lookout for-- will determine how you evaluate the potential of a property.

Of course, location plays a large role in the desirability of a property. The neighborhood it is located in might have some negative impact, whether it is next to a school, or a manufacturing plant makes a big difference.

What does the neighborhood look like as you are coming upon the house? Look at the house itself... what does the roof look like? Exterior, windows, landscaping, accessibility, handicapped accessible? Inside, start in the basement, check the foundation, furnace, hot water tank, water supply coming into the house. Is there a well, septic system, city water, sewer, old electrical service, new service?

When you are looking, analyze everything, from the roof to the basement.

Make a cursory exam for termites or other insects by examining the wood in the basement. Are there any mud tunnels, chewed wood? Check for mold in the basement.

Going from room to room, scan the room from top to bottom. The kitchen and bathrooms should be up to date. Anticipate updating if necessary. That could impact the price of rent, or resale value. Style doesn't matter much but contemporary houses bring in higher rents than a colonial, cape cod or bungalow.

The paint should be good and clean as should be the carpeting. Look for hardwood floors under existing carpet. In the long run refinished hardwood floors outlast carpet.

Take a look at the layout of the house and traffic patterns. Functionally obsolescent houses include layouts that are impractical, such as bedrooms with access through a bathroom, or walk-through bedrooms.

The best way to acquire talent needed to analyze property is to go on a bus tour with your REIA group. Look at 5-7 houses with experienced investors who can explain what needs to be done in an analytical process. You want someone there to help you determine the profitability of a potential purchase.

Don't forget to use your team to help you evaluate properties. Take an expert in the field of rehabbing to walk through and estimate rehab costs. Take a realtor to evaluate how much you could resell for, or a fellow investor who is familiar with the area to help you determine how much you could rent it for. Don't be afraid to ask a fellow investor to come with you. Seek their advice and counsel if you can and if need be, take one or two with you to look at the house, offer to pay them a small fee for their time and effort. There are few things investors would rather do than look at houses.

Remember that your profit is made at the time of purchase and not at the time of sale. If you don't know how to do it, find those who do so they can mentor you in that process. Surround yourself with fellow investors. It is worth it to hire a home inspector and a fellow investor can recommend a good and reliable one.

Are you going to buy every house at the right price? No, but hopefully you won't buy too many at the wrong price. In normal times if you make a mistake, and you wait long enough, real estate will bail you out of your problem, price-wise.

It is important that you know what you want. Do you want single units, multi-units, commercial? Do you want to wholesale? Rehab? Hold and rent?

Is there any particular area that is better than the other? No. Remain open so that you can change periodically. You may find yourself supplementing your usual menu with a different location, style or price range.

The biggest thing to consider is where your comfort zone is and how many times you should you go outside of your comfort zone to accomplish more than you thought you might do.

After being in the business for a while you will mix a number of these things together, the important thing is to keep active, do something, experiment once in a while with something different. Go outside of your comfort zone.

Take a challenge offered by a fellow investor sometime. My own motivation is sometimes kicked into gear by a comment made by a fellow investor. Find out what they are doing in their field, get their comments, find out if that is an area you care to deal in. Just keep on pursuing whatever in an aggressive manner and you will be successful no matter what style of house you pick or what your exit strategy is.

Keys to My Success

We all know that one of the key components to being successful is having a good support system. Nothing is more important in real estate. Show me a spouse who is opposed to your acquiring real estate, and I will show you a real estate investor who will have much greater difficulty making it.

Although I can't say that my wife, Deloris, was ever a vocal cheerleader of my serial real estate acquisitions, she never discouraged me. She may have complained when I turned a deaf ear to her requests for new carpet in our home because I was working on a deal, but all in all, she knows how passionate I am about what I do and wants me to be happy.

If you are single and get involved with someone, make sure they are on board with your strategy. If at a future date you comingle your finances, your significant other needs to be made aware of what the future holds—to whatever extent you know yourself. If you have a life-partner and you decide to get involved in real estate, take the time to share your passion with them. Take

time now to make it happen before it becomes a bone
of contention and you lose your relationship over it. If
you are truly bitten by the real estate bug, you can't get
away from it, so take special care in preparing your
partner for the road ahead.

I think that another reason I have been successful is
that I always try to act with a keen sense of integrity.
I buy at a fair price—not to say that I don't look for
a bargain—and I resell at fair market value. If I find
out that a fellow investor made an offer on a property
I am interested in, I won't try to outbid him. There
are enough properties out there that we don't need to
compete against investors we know.

Remain flexible and open to changing strategies.
Although there really is no bad time to invest in real
estate, different times can call for different approaches.
Government regulations can limit the things you can do
with your property, how you deal with your tenants, or
how you maintain your properties. Changing interest
rates or local economic atmospheres can influence the
rate at which you acquire properties.

Do your due diligence. Point of sale inspections may be
coming to your neck of the woods. You may be required
to hook up to city sewer systems or water hook ups
upon transfer of title. Your property can be included in
a flood zone, which can require purchasing expensive
flood policies. The EPA can require that you keep your

property dimly lit to avoid confusing the turtles that may nest on your property, or keep quiet so as not to disturb a bald eagle's nest.

Get involved in legislation that involves real estate investing. The laws that govern our livelihood can have a great impact on our future, so it is important that we look out for our own interests by including our input in the drafting of local laws. How do you do that? By getting involved in the election process with financial contributions to like minded candidates. You can even work on their individual campaigns and share with your acquaintances and business associates your candidate's positions. Attend your local governmental meetings and get to know your local elected officials. Invite them to attend and address your REIA group. Show them how valuable an asset investors are to the community and economy.

Two of the rules I live by have to do with my religious beliefs: leave Sundays for the Lord's work and stay current on your tithings. The few open houses I held on a Sunday confirmed that I could sell just as many houses in six days as others did in seven. Every time I receive a check I write down ten percent of that amount on a piece of paper. This tithing and additional offerings is what I will give to my church for the Lord's work.

Give free advice. Taking the time to meet with new investors and giving them advice is a great way to not only help people but also groom investors who might borrow from me and make me money. Some people believe they shouldn't give their secrets away, but I think that education is the key to being successful, and the more you share, the more you will benefit in the long run.

This Is Not A Negative Book

Even though there are lots of opportunities to lose money, there are plenty of opportunities to make money. You have to learn how to overcome problems, and learn from your mistakes because they can become very valuable lessons.

It is my desire to see anybody and everyone who wants to get into real estate to succeed in accomplishing their objective. It can be an exciting, rewarding, unique and non boring job, which, if you love it, you will not call a job, but a loving adventure. A labor of love.

I have mentored over the years 30 people who have achieved some level of success. Some of them I don't know how or whether I influenced them. I talk, kick them out and I throw them in the water and tell them to start swimming, tell them to not drown, even though there is a lifeguard standing by.

Before you even purchase real estate, you need to think of what your exit strategy might be. There are multiple exit strategies available, and if you don't have one you will be stuck like within a building that catches on fire. If you don't plan an exit strategy on your acquisitions, you will burn up like in a fire.

Exit strategies include:

1. buy and hold: turning into a rental

2. buy and wholesale

3. buy and do a retail sale

All or none of these could involve a certain degree of updating, rehabbing, or sprucing up. That's where some of your exit strategies can determine the amount of rehabbing you want to do on your property. It is best to have several exit strategies on each property.

If I purchase a property with the intention of retailing or wholesaling it, my personal belief is that if I can't sell it within three to four months, I will change my strategy to one of converting it to a rental or a land contract sale.

I can minimize my loss by putting it into my own stable of rentals. As I mentioned previously, in order to lose a lot less money, you can always pull equity out of a house to use it to get your cash back. So you don't want to be in a position to have poor credit in case you want to refinance the properties using a conventional lender.

Use your exit strategy to turn any negative into a positive.

While I may not make an immediate profit, I can rent out my property to receive all the benefits of an income producing property. If there is a need to recover some cash that was put into the deal you can use your equity in the property to get a loan. Just keep in mind that you don't want to leverage everything too highly.

Working with other peoples' money is a good thing to do, but you don't want to use too much of other peoples' money and find out that you can't pay it back someday.

How to pull equity out of your properties...

Keep trying until you find a lender willing to lend out on a property. There is someone out there if you are a credit-worthy borrower and your properties are sufficient to appraise. Don't forget to look at private parties for funding.

It is very difficult to get more than four loans out of most banking institutions, because they package the loans for the secondary market. Banks that put your loan into their own portfolio can loan on any number of properties they choose.

There is no better investment than real estate. What is more exciting, reading a prospectus on a company or looking at a house? Getting an insurance policy that pays you off when you're dead or something that pays you while you are alive? Do you know what it feels like to make money while you are sleeping? Or while you are sick and not able to work? It's not a job, if you love what you are doing, and there is nothing better than doing what you love.

www.ingramcontent.com/pod-product-compliance
Lightning Source LLC
Chambersburg PA
CBHW021904170526
45157CB00005B/1954